MW00957891

SMALL-RV NINJA

RV Maintenance for New Road Warriors

ROBIN NORTH

SMALL - RV NINJA

RV Maintenance for New Road Warriors

ROBIN NORTH

WWW.BEACHNANA.COM

iii

Copyright ©2018 Robin North

All rights reserved.

ISBN: 9781791780746

Dedication

Every book has a spark and the ignition point for Small-RV Ninja is the RV adventure I have had with my husband, Jim. His unending patience with all we had to learn, his willingness to drive while I wrote, and his talent to keep me laughing when RV problems appeared, made our traveling lifestyle so much fun.

Thanks Jim, for all you do and all the great times ahead on the road!

Table of Contents

About This Book

Why Small-RV Ninja?

My grandkids love to watch the Ninja Warrior Challenge TV show and, in fact, it inspired them to design an obstacle course on our last beach vacation. Each of the kids was so excited to play "ninja warrior" and quite proud when they completed the entire obstacle course. They learned to overcome a lot of different challenges in order to claim the title.

The TV show's title is inspired by the Ninja's of history. They were masters of espionage and often disguised themselves to accomplish their tasks. To be successful in their disguises, they became acquainted with many different jobs and the specialized knowledge required of each.

I thought about all my husband and I have learned since purchasing our small RV a few years ago. We have worn a lot of hats troubleshooting issues and understanding how to maintain our RV. We've learned everything from how the plumbing works to leveling the unit. Surely, those who learn so many different jobs and acquire so much specialized knowledge about RVs might be considered a "ninja" – *a Small-RV Ninja!*

Hence the title of this book. A Small-RV Ninja needs to know a little bit about a lot of things. From basic electrical systems, plumbing, heating and air conditioning, to basic chassis care. A Small-RV Ninja has to school themselves in whatever they need to know to care for their RV.

Why I wrote this book

And when I say "a little about a lot of things" I am defining the scope of this book! There are many good books written on using and maintaining your RV. Some are quite technical or have detailed explanations that go far beyond any question I could even think to ask. But they tend to be very general in order to include as many different types of RVs as possible.

That said, since they address so many different types of RVs, it's hard to tell what information applies to your RV. It takes knowing your RV to recognize what applies. So, how do you learn enough about your RV to sort through all that information?

Well, it makes sense to first explore your RV manufacturer's website and documentation. In our quest to learn about our own RV, we found there are many similarities among the small motorcoach-style RVs. Enough similarities that it seemed reasonable to attempt a more specific reference for them.

I am not an engineer, an electrician or a plumber. I am an RV owner who needed some basic information on how my vehicle works and what to do to take care of it so that I don't inadvertently damage it.

After many mistakes and wading through many books and articles trying to find answers about my RV, I decided to write an easy reference for beginning

RVers. Something they can use without being overwhelmed by what they don't yet know – and particular to small RVs rather than trying to include every size.

This whole book is dedicated to RVs in the Class B+ to small Class C motorhomes. We don't address tow-behinds or fifth wheels, nor do we attempt to include larger Class C or Class A coaches.

With that in mind, you'll soon realize this book is not all-inclusive. It is a basic treatment of what you need to know about your small RV to maintain it and to troubleshoot a problem. For instance, if there is no water from your RV kitchen faucet, you'll know to check the water level in your holding tank, make sure the water pump's working, or make sure the city-water connection is turned on.

There is also the matter of proper maintenance. Your RV is a huge investment so you'll want to maintain it. Knowing what needs regular maintenance and what that maintenance entails will go a long way to keeping your RV functional. Some things you can do yourself with very little effort, other maintenance items are best left to professionals. Often one system impacts another, so having a regular maintenance routine will help you stay on top of issues before they become problems.

Bonus Resources

To that end, I've prepared a couple of bonus items for you to use along with this book. The first is a maintenance schedule; A simple file that you can use to track all the maintenance items for your RV. The second is a note sheet to keep all the numbers and information about your RV in a single place.

Both of these tools are included at the end of this book. This puts all your RV information at your fingertips. If you prefer to print out a copy of these resources, you can download .pdf copies from our website: https://www.beachnana.com/bonus-content-srvn .

Introduction

It's often love-at-first-sight with RVs. You see its lines, its color scheme, and its stance calling you to travel. We often purchase an RV because of its chassis. Whether you prefer the large luxury of a class "A" or the flexibility and simple appointments of a class "B" conversion van, it's the RV chassis that speaks to us first.

But then it's the engine that draws our attention. How much power for hill climbing, torque for towing, and economy of fuel use does the engine offer? It's the combination of chassis and engine – specific to each model – that sends us on the hunt to find the right RV for us.

Eventually, as we narrow down the options, we begin to seek out the creature comforts of the interior and all the little "extras" that will make one RV model stand above all the others as our perfect traveling companion.

But an RV is more than the sum of its parts. It provides a platform for experiences near and far. It provides a comfortable and familiar place to rest and relax. It provides the sense of freedom to go whenever and where ever we wish – as long as there's a road ahead. No matter where your travels take you, you carry a place to call home.

Some RVs offer extravagant space and features, others more modest accommodations. We will focus on the smaller RVs for this book, though many of the principals we discuss can be scaled up for Class A or Super C units.

Smaller RVs are a fast-growing segment of the RV market yet, when we purchased our 25-foot Class B+ unit, there was not much information available. We had a lot of questions about these smaller RVs but had to wade through books and articles that covered all sizes and types.

This year, after so many questions from our blog readers, we decided to share what we've learned and experienced as small-RV owners – and first time RV owners.

Overall, our small unit is both comfortable and flexible. We've enjoyed trips lasting two weeks or two months in its small space. And, if we were willing to downsize appropriately, it could accommodate a full-time lifestyle!

In the following pages, we will take a tour of a small RV and look at each major system and its primary components. This will help give you a better idea of how all the parts work together for your comfort and safety on the road and at the campground.

Then we'll wrap it up with a few practical tips for using your small RV. Included are two checklists for setting up and breaking down a campsite at either a standard campground or when boondocking (that means, without electrical or water hook-ups).

Finally, we have created two tools to help you keep track of RV maintenance and all the important numbers and information about your RV. You will find them at the back of this book, or you can download a .pdf copy of them from our blog, at www.beachnana.com/bonus-content-srvn.

Many RV dealers give you a brief walk-through to help you learn where everything is located in your RV. If you're new to RVing, this can be quite overwhelming. So much information in a very short time!

To help you absorb the information at a more relaxed pace, we'll use this book to take a tour of your RV. Along the way we will indicate what items you should note down in your bonus RV Notebook or on the RV Maintenance Schedule (did you download them yet?).

Each system section covers how the system works as well as all of its related components. Understanding the relationship between system components is invaluable when troubleshooting a problem. When you know the components of each system and how they work together, it is easier to pinpoint a malfunction.

Even if you can't fix it, you will have a bit more confidence discussing it with your service professional. Each section also includes a few tips you need to know about the system and/or its care.

Now, let's start your Small-RV Ninja training!

A Walk-Through of Your RV

A Ninja Surveys the Territory

Step right in. Take a slow and careful look around as you walk through the door of your coach. As a ninja-in-training, there are a few things you want to locate both inside and outside the coach. Obviously, you want to find the switches for lighting and other systems but you'll also want to locate actual components for maintenance.

As we talk about each system, we will use this mark (**) to prompt you to make a note of important information in your RV Maintenance Schedule (RVMS) or in your RV Information Notebook (RVIN) you downloaded earlier. If you haven't downloaded them yet, you can get them from our website, Beach Nana Travels at https://www.beachnana.com/bonus-content-srvn .

Safety Equipment

Ninjas Know Their Limits

Safety equipment should be easy to spot. A ninja has to consider potential danger so identifying safety equipment is the first step to minimizing risk. It's important that you know where each safety item and alarm is located so when an alarm goes off you know which one is sounding!

Fire Extinguisher

** Make a note of the serial number and the expiration date (RVMS)

Every RV is equipped with a fire extinguisher. Make sure you know its location and how to use it. If you are unsure, ask your local fire department for help on how to use a fire extinguisher.

There will be an expiration date on the extinguisher indicating when it needs to be recharged or replaced. Make a habit of checking it before every trip.

Smoke and CO Detector

** Make a note of the type of battery it takes (RVMS)

In such a small space these safety monitors are a must. They can detect tiny particles of smoke and/or carbon monoxide in the air and sound an alarm to alert you. Most detectors need a battery and will begin to "chirp" as the battery runs low. You'll have to replace the battery to stop the "chirping" so make sure you keep an extra on hand. The alarm sound is piercingly loud so it is unlikely you'd sleep through it or mistake it for the chirping!

LP Detector

*** Make a note of its expiration date (RVMS) and a note of its make and model number (RVIN)*

Liquid Propane is quite flammable and is odorless. A "rotten egg" smell is added to it so you have some indication of a leak. If you smell a bad odor, or if the LP alarm goes off, leave the RV immediately and let it air out. It's a good idea to open a window when using a propane appliance like a stove – just in case!

Although the LP monitors can be a lifesaver, they also have a shelf-life. Check the date stamped on the unit and plan on replacing it every two to five years. Unfortunately, you may not realize it needs replacing until it begins triggering false alarms. Treat every LP monitor alarm as an emergency and turn off the propane at its source. But if yours is alarming frequently, have a service professional inspect the system for leaks and consider replacing the monitor.

Each of these monitors and alarms are critical for your safety. Do not disable them. An RV is such a small space that you need every second to get out in an emergency. Keep them clean by wiping the dust away with a soft, damp cloth.

It's a good idea to test the alarms periodically to be sure they are functional and have them serviced according to the manufacturer's recommendations.

Systems Monitor Panel

A Ninja Monitors the Situation

This is a small-RV ninja's "command central". The systems monitor panel gives you a quick recap of the state of your RV systems. Some newer RV models use a tablet for this information. Others use a standard wall-mounted panel. Either way, the Systems Monitor Panel should include the following:

Holding Tanks (monitors the level for fresh water, gray, and black tanks)

Inverter Switch (to turn the inverter on and off)

Battery Charge Indicator (monitors the batteries for charge level)

Switch for the Generator (to turn generator on and off - if you have one)

Solar Panel Status Indicator (shows level of solar panel production)

Switch for the Water Heater (you do want a hot shower, right?)

Switch for the Water Pump (to turn on and off the water pump)

The various monitors let you know when to fill the fresh water tank and empty the gray and blank tanks. The battery indicator will let you know when the battery charge is running low and needs to be recharged. One monitor will indicate the number of hours on the generator so you know when to perform maintenance, and there should be a set of switches to tell you whether or not the inverter, generator, water pump, and water heater are turned on.

In all, the monitor panel is an essential component in your RV. You'll find yourself checking it before, during and after every trip. Maintenance on the panel is best left to professionals. ** *Make a note of the model and make (RVIN)*

Liquid Propane System

Ninjas Fuel the Fun

You may be surprised that liquid Propane is the preferred fuel to operate several components of the RV. As an RV ninja, you will learn it is the backup fuel for a dual-fuel refrigerator and it also fuels the furnace, gas cooktop, and the water heater. Additionally, it may fuel the generator (these can be fueled by propane or diesel) and some RVs have the option of having an outlet to attach a barbecue grill. Now that's some ninja fun!

The LP tank is located on the exterior of the RV and, as long as the LP tank valve is turned to "on", most of the appliances that use the LP will work automatically. (Your RV documentation will indicate which appliances use LP and if they require a pilot to be lit or if the pilot is electronic.) The propane valve will also have a pressure regulator to maintain a constant flow of LP to all of your appliances.

Since so many appliances use propane you will need to refill the tank sooner or later. Most hardware stores, propane dealers, and some campgrounds sell propane, so it is relatively easy to find. And, when you need a fill-up for your propane tank, they will do the job for you. Because you need a license to dispense propane, there are no self-serve propane pumps!

Propane tanks are installed either horizontally or vertically and they must stay in the orientation in which they are installed, otherwise the flow of LP to the RV systems will be compromised.

A word of warning about LP: there is a chemical added to propane to make it easier to detect a leak. If you smell something like rotten eggs or onions, it may be a propane leak. Leave the RV immediately and let it air out. Turn off the propane valve at the tank and get a service professional to inspect the system.

Liquid Propane Tips:

- The propane typically runs your stove, your heat, your hot water heater, generator, and grill.
- There is "cold weather" propane and "warm weather" propane. The cold weather variety is a bit more expensive and is used, as the name implies, in cold weather climates. The type you buy will depend on where you are when you purchase it (cold climate or warm climate). Both types function the same way.
- You can have the LP tank filled at most well-equipped hardware stores or propane dealers. Although you need a license to dispense propane it doesn't hurt to ask if the attendant is familiar with filling RV LP tanks.
- A full propane tank is only 80% full. Any more than that could be dangerous since propane expands.

- An LP leak is dangerous. Every RV should be equipped with an LP detector. If the alarm has sounded, leave the RV immediately and let the RV air out. Turn off the propane at the tank and then have a service professional check the system.

Have your propane system checked by a service professional every two years.

*** Make a note how often to service (RVMS)*

The Small-RV Electrical System

A Ninja Knows His Power Source

As a novice ninja, I regarded electricity as almost magic. You flip a switch and there is light, or coffee, or music! I never gave much thought to how it works - until I bought an RV. My very first RV troubleshooting adventure began with electricity. I flipped a switch and nothing happened – no lights, no coffee, no music. Now what?

My home has a fuse panel, so I looked for that first. Found it! – But no problems there. The batteries were charged so all good there too.

After diligently searching through the manuals and, in desperation, calling the manufacturer, the service technician told me about the inverter "reset" button.

I didn't even know that we had an inverter, where it was or what it did. With a little guidance from the tech, I found it, hit the reset button and the electricity was restored. Magic!

Understanding the components of the electrical system, how each works, and how they work together may take some of the "magic" out of the electrical system but it makes me feel a lot more capable to troubleshoot problems.

Here's what you need to know...

Electrical System Components List

Battery Bank for the coach

** *Note how many batteries and what type (RVIN) age of battery (RVMS)*

Inverter

** *Note the model number and make (RVIN) and recommended maintenance (RVMS)*

Fuse Panel

** *Make a note of the types of fuses to keep on hand (RVIN)*

Solar Panels (if you have them)

** *Note the number of panels, the model and make (RVIN) and recommended maintenance (RVMS)*

Generator (if you have one)

** *Note the model number and make (RVIN) and recommended maintenance (RVMS)*

How the RV electrical system works

An RV's electrical system is made up of several players: the coach battery bank, the inverter/converter, the generator, and solar panels. Your RV may not have all of these components but will most certainly have at least the battery bank and inverter.

To get power to all your RV appliances and systems you have a few choices: shore power (that's just nifty name for an electrical outlet at home or at a campground outlet), an onboard generator, or your RV coach battery bank.

Inverter

Using power in an RV from batteries requires the use of the inverter. Most newer RVs include a converting feature with the inverter that allows it to recharge the battery bank.

The inverter takes the stored DC power from the batteries and inverts it to AC power that is used by your appliances. This is particularly important when you are boondocking, away from a shore power source.

In its converting mode, the inverter takes the AC shore or generator power and converts it to DC power to be stored in the battery bank. This is an automatic process, so you don't typically have to give it much thought. Plug into shore power and the battery bank starts charging up. Or, switch on the generator and the battery bank charges up.

Be sure you keep the area around the inverter clear so that air can circulate freely. Other than keeping the area around the inverter clean and free of debris, there is not much DIY maintenance but do make a note in your maintenance schedule to have it checked by a professional yearly.

Inverter Tips

- The inverter allows designated outlets and some appliances to work when not plugged into shore power. It transforms DC battery power to AC usable power for the RV outlets and appliances.

- To use the inverter when boondocking, find the inverter "on-off" switch located in the systems monitoring panel and simply switch it to "on". When you are finished, turn it to the "off" position.
- There is not much maintenance for the inverter, but you can make sure it has plenty of room around it for air circulation and keep the air intake vents clear of debris.
- Only use the inverter when boondocking and not when plugged into shore power.
- Keep in mind you won't be able to use all of your electrical appliances when using battery power and the inverter. There is a limit to their capacity so the big appliances like microwave ovens, air conditioners, and sometimes even coffee makers may require the use of shore or generator power.

Shore Power

Shore power allows you to run everything in your RV from the air conditioner to your television. You plug in the RV to the campground electrical outlet and your RV is ready for action. Behind the scenes the AC current from the campground hook-up is transferred to your RV appliances and outlets through the inverter.

If your inverter is equipped with a converter, the shore power will also re-charge the battery bank. Not all small RVs have an inverter with this battery-charging function, but most newer RVs do have it. You'll have to check your RV documentation to find out if yours has this feature.

There are several types of electrical supply current at a campground: 15, 20, 30, and 50-amp service. You need to know which type of service your RV uses. Bigger RVs typically use 50-amp service and smaller RVs, such as our 25-foot Sprinter, use 30-amp service. (You can find this information in your RV documentation).

So, what do you do when the outlets don't match your RV's amperage? Outlet adapters come to the rescue. They adapt the plug from your RV's amperage to what is available at the campsite hook-up. For instance, these adapters allow you to use a 50-amp outlet with a 30-amp RV plug. Just attach the adapter to the plug on your RV power cord or to the end of your surge protector, and voila! Bob's your uncle- all good!

When plugging in to shore power, use a surge protector. This will protect your RV from electricity surges that could "fry" your RV electrical system. We found out how important the surge protector was when camping during a thunderstorm. Lightening hit the campground and burned out our surge protector but that saved our RV. It did its job admirably. We found the nearest RV supply and bought another one the next day!

Most surge protectors include a polarity tester that will indicate a faulty circuit. When you plug in the surge protector to the campsite power, a set of lights will indicate "green" if it's safe. If there is an issue with the shore power hookup the lights will indicate yellow or red. If that happens, report it to the campground and find another campsite.

1. To actually hook up to the shore power, follow this safe sequence:

2. Turn off the power at the campsite box and plug in your surge protector (just the surge protector - without the RV power cord).

3. Turn on the power at the box and check the lights on the surge protector. If they are all green, you can continue hooking up.

4. Turn off the power at the box again.

5. Connect the power cord to the RV first, then to the surge protector, then to the campsite electrical box.

6. Turn on the power at the box, recheck the surge protector lights to make sure they are still green and you're ready to camp!

Shore Power Tips

- Buy a surge protector and use it every time you plug into shore power. This will protect your RV from electricity surges that could "fry" your electrical system.

- Follow the safe sequence outlined above when hooking up to shore power. Always start with the campsite power switched to the "off" position.

- Before you plug into shore power, always test the campground electrical outlet. Most surge protectors will indicate a faulty circuit with a series of red or yellow lights. If it's all green, it's all good!

- If your surge protector indicates a fault with yellow or red lights, report it to the campground office and find a new site.

- It's also a good idea to invest in a couple of outlet adapters. If you find yourself at a campsite with only one shore power outlet and it isn't the size you need, an adapter can save the day

Battery Power

The batteries allow you to use some of your appliances when you are boondocking without a shore power hookup. In this case, your RV gets power from the battery bank. The inverter draws DC current from the batteries and inverts it to AC current for your appliances and outlets. That inverter is a handy little device! Of course, the battery bank must be charged up for the inverter to draw power.

There are two sets of batteries in your RV. One set in the engine compartment for the business side of the RV, and one set in the "house" side for all the electronic needs of the "house". The house batteries on a small RV are typically two, deep cycle batteries that need to be monitored and recharged when the charge drops to 12.5 volts.

If you allow the charge to drop below 12.5, the chance of battery damage increases. Little crystals form on the battery plates rendering them useless. Some slight damage can be repaired, but more severe cases require replacing the battery.

You can recharge the batteries by plugging into shore power, using your generator, or using a stand-alone battery charger. Most of the newer small-RVs are equipped with a converter function that allow the batteries to be recharged when plugged into shore power.

You will also need to check the water level in the batteries periodically – even when you are not using your RV. Top off the water level to just cover the plates and use ONLY distilled water. Tap water can reduce the life of the battery. If your batteries are the sealed type, you do not need to add water and are considered maintenance free.

Finally, it's a good idea to switch the house batteries to "off" or disconnect them when not using your RV. This keeps the batteries from dropping to a dangerous low charge level. Even if everything is turned off in the coach, there is always some power draw and turning off the batteries is the only way to stop that draw.

Battery Tips

- The water level in the batteries needs to be checked and refilled regularly - unless you have the sealed type. If your RV batteries are the sealed type there is no maintenance required.
- When adding water to the batteries, use only distilled water. Tap water can reduce the life of your RV's deep cycle batteries.
- Monitor the level of the batteries' charge. It needs to stay at 50% or above. For most small-RV applications, that means the charge level should not drop below 12.5 volts.

- If you see that the battery level has dropped, either start the generator to re-charge the batteries, start the engine of the RV to help re-charge them (this is not terribly effective though), plug into shore power, or you can take the batteries out of the coach and hook them up to a battery charger.
- There is usually a battery disconnect switch for the 'house' batteries. When you are not using your RV, it is a good idea to switch the battery to the off or "disconnect" position to preserve battery life.

Solar Panel Power

If you have them, solar panels transmit the power they generate from the sun to re-charge the battery bank. They don't typically generate enough power to run your whole coach but just enough to keep the battery bank topped up.

Solar panels are installed on the roof of a small-RV and they have a charge monitor inside the RV. If you are boondocking, solar panels can be a great help, providing free power as long as the sun is shining. You will, of course, have to monitor how much power you are using vs the amount being delivered by the solar panels. As the sun fades into evening, you'll only have the power stored in the battery bank for the overnight hours, so use that power wisely!

Solar Panel Tips

- Keep them clean! Sitting up on the roof and out of sight it's easy to forget about the solar panels. They will be more efficient if you keep them clear of debris and clean them regularly. See your manufacturer's recommendations on cleaning and servicing.

- If you are boondocking, monitor the amount of power delivered by the solar panels vs your usage to keep the battery bank topped up, especially as the sun goes down.

Generator Power

A Generator can do two things: either re-charge the battery bank through a converter or supply AC current to your appliances and outlets through the inverter. You can run almost all your appliances and air conditioner on the generator's power (but probably not all at once!). If you plan to boondock frequently, a generator is a "must-have" item.

RV generators are either diesel or propane fueled. They are noisy and emit noxious fumes, so are not particularly welcomed in campgrounds. Use them thoughtfully to not disturb other campers (run them during the day to recharge batteries or run appliances for short periods).

Like most motors, generators need to be run occasionally with a "load" to keep them in tip top shape. That means to gradually add power draw, run at that level for a while, and then gradually decrease the power draw before shutting the generator down.

For example, start up the generator and let it run for a couple of minutes without any appliances running. Once it has a few minutes to warm up, turn on the air conditioner or run the microwave oven to add a power draw or "load". Run the appliance for a few minutes and then turn it off. Let the generator run without load for a few more minutes before shutting it down.

In all, the run time might be about fifteen minutes. The amount of load and the time required to "exercise" your generator may vary so check your documentation for the manufacturer's recommendations.

There should be a generator section in the monitor panel that indicates the number of hours the generator has been used. Maintenance on the generator is predicated on the number of hours run. Check your manufacturer's recommendations for how often to service your generator and what needs to be done.

Usually changing the fuel filter is all most of us want to tackle, so the more in-depth servicing can be left to a professional. Just keep track of the number of hours on your generator and make a note in your maintenance schedule about when to service it.

Generator Tips

- Some RVs are equipped with a generator for producing electricity while boondocking. A generator can be either diesel powered or propane powered. It can provide electricity for the coach appliances and air conditioner and can charge the coach battery through the converter (not all RVs have this option).
- The generator will run most of the RV "house" electrical needs if you don't have shore power. But it tends to be quite noisy.

- For safety, do not run the generator while sleeping since even a tiny propane leak could produce dangerous fumes inside your RV.
- A generator needs to be run on a regular basis to keep the fuel lines clean as well as the carburetor or fuel injectors. A best practice is to run it with a "load" at least once a week. Turn it on and, once it is warmed up (wait a few minutes), turn on the air conditioner and let it run for ten or fifteen minutes.
- When finished with a generator, first turn off the "load" appliance and let it cycle off. Then run the generator without any load for a few minutes before shutting down. A gradual "unloading" prevents damage.
- Check your manufacturer's recommendations on regular maintenance like changing the spark plugs, filters and oil.
- Generators are noisy and emit carbon monoxide, so be courteous to your neighbors and don't run your generator at night or for prolonged periods. This is particularly important in a close-quarters campground where you are sharing space with tent campers. Think of the generator like a noisy, barking dog!
- Since a generator emits carbon monoxide, make sure the exhaust is not wafting back into the RV. Your CO detector should go off if there are dangerous levels in the RV, but take precautions to make sure the exhaust is properly directed.

The Small-RV Plumbing System

A Clean Ninja is a Happy Ninja

A ninja on the road is always looking for their next long, hot shower. Campground bath houses are fine but there's nothing like having your own shower with your own ninja shower accessories!

Plumbing System Components List

Water Heater

**Make a note of the model number and make (RVIN)

Water Pump

**Make a note of the model number and make (RVIN)

Service Bay

Holding Tanks

Sinks, Shower, and Toilet

Water pressure regulator

** Make a note of the model number and make (RVIN)

Water filter

**Make a note of the model number and make (RVIN) Also, note initial installation and schedule regular filter changes (RVMS)

How the RV plumbing system works

RVs have pretty straight-forward plumbing systems. Fresh water comes from either a campground faucet hook-up (usually termed "city water") or the onboard fresh water holding tank. Waste water exits the RV into either the gray (water from sink and shower drains) or black (toilet) holding tanks. When the tanks are full, you empty them at a dump station.

Holding Tank Monitor

RVs usually have an electronic tank monitor panel where you can see the level in each of the fresh, gray, and black holding tanks. This lets you know when to add fresh water and/or when you need to empty the gray and black holding tanks.

Realistically, there are a few more things you will need to know. Let's start at the beginning – getting water into your RV.

Using a City Water Connection

Most RV campgrounds have a city water connection. It's a faucet at your campsite which allows you to connect your RV to a city water supply. Attach a fresh water hose to the campsite faucet and then attach the other end to the "city water" intake on your RV. This will be the water source you use when at an RV resort or campground.

Note: you do not use the water pump when connected to city water. The pressure from the city water connection will be enough to pump water through the RV's system.

Using a Water Pressure Regulator

A city water hook-up is a wonderful convenience when camping – and you won't run out of water! However, the pressure of city water can be overpowering for an RV's small plumbing system. So, it's wise to attach a water pressure regulator to your RV water hose at the campsite faucet connection end. Make sure to purchase one that has a gauge and an adjustment valve. It will give a reading of the city water pressure at the campsite faucet and allow you to adjust the pressure of the water going to your RV. Your RV's documentation will dictate a safe water pressure for your model RV. (If your documentation does not specify a pressure, 50 – 60 psi is considered safe.)

Using a Water filter

And, since you probably won't be checking on water quality everywhere you camp, a water filter attached to your RV's water hose is also a good idea. It works like any water filter used in the home to filter out chemicals and particulates in the water supply (i.e., lead, contaminants, and microorganisms). Make sure to change the filter regularly.

The Onboard Fresh Water Holding Tank

If you don't have a city water connection because you're "boondocking" (camping in a wilderness area or overnighting in a shopping center parking lot) you'll need to use your onboard fresh water tank.

First, make sure there is water in your fresh water holding tank. Some RVs have a hose connection that you simply attach to an outdoor faucet at home or in a campground to fill the water tank. Others have a syphon-type of arrangement to draw water from a container into the tank.

To fill it, connect a fresh water hose to the fresh water intake valve in the service bay, then connect the other end of the hose to a fresh water faucet at home or at a campground. Depending on your set-up, you may need to turn a valve on the RV to direct water to the fresh water holding tank. Others have a special port for this single purpose, ready to connect a hose.

Check the monitor panel and find the indicator assigned to the fresh water tank. As you fill the fresh water tank, monitor the level so you don't overfill it.

The Water Pump

But just having water in the tank doesn't mean you have water at the RV kitchen sink. You'll need to switch on the water pump to move the fresh water from the tank to the plumbing lines. In a small RV the water pump is small too, often tucked under a sink or in a cabinet. It runs on electrical power from the coach battery bank.

The water pump can be quite noisy as it charges the lines, but will quiet down when the lines are filled with water. You may hear it go on and off as you use water from the tank since it's pumping water into the lines to replace what you use.

The water pump will supply fresh water to the sink faucets, the shower, the hot water heater, and the toilet. Keep an eye on your fresh water tank level. You'll have to monitor your water use so that you don't run out of water or run the water pump "dry". Running the water pump without water can damage the motor.

To use the water in the holding tank, you'll turn on the water pump, give it a minute to fill the plumbing lines, and turn on the faucet or use the toilet. It may sputter a bit if there is air in the lines and you'll hear the "whirring" of the water pump as you use water. For hot water, you'll need to let the water heater fill, turn it on, and wait for it to heat the water.

Water Pump Maintenance Tips

- After each travel season, remove and clean the filter on the intake side of the water pump.

**Make a note for maintenance (RVMS)*

- Sanitize the pump (and the whole plumbing system) at least once each year to prevent algae growth. (see instructions later in this chapter)

**Make a note for maintenance (RVMS)*

The Water Heater

There are two types of water heaters in today's small RVs. The first, is the standard, six-gallon propane and/or electric water heater which works like the one in your home. It heats a tank of water and, as you use it, it refills with cold water. If you use more than the six gallons, you'll run out of hot water and must wait while the fresh supply is heated.

The standard six-gallon water heater allows two short showers without running out of hot water. Recovery time varies, but our experience has been pretty consistent with less than 20 minutes for full heat recovery between uses.

Most of the standard water heaters come equipped with an electronic ignition. You flip a switch inside the RV and the water heater pilot ignites. If your RV doesn't have this feature, you will have to light the pilot manually after your RV is parked and leveled.

The second type of water heater is the tankless variety. It creates a continuous flow of hot water on demand. It has a very small container of heated water and, when you turn on the hot water tap, it signals the tankless water heater to heat the water flowing through its system. By the time the initial supply is used, the burners are heating the flowing water sufficiently.

Tankless water heaters can be powered by either electricity or propane and, in fact, use less propane than the standard water heater since there is no big tank of water to keep hot.

Regardless of which type of water heater you have, the length of a shower is determined more by the capacity of the gray holding tank than by the water heater's capacity!

Water Heater Maintenance Tips

- Read up on the safety features that are installed on your water heater.
- For a standard water heater, you may have an anode that helps prevent corrosion of the tank. It will need to be inspected and replace it when it is corroded. ** *Make a note for maintenance (RVMS)*
- When using the water heater for the first time or after it has been winterized, you will need to fill it with water before igniting. DO NOT RUN A WATER HEATER WITHOUT WATER!
- To fill a standard water heater, turn the bypass valve to "normal" and turn on the city water. (if boondocking, turn on the water pump in the RV to draw water from the fresh water holding tank). Open the hot water tap in the RV and you will hear the tank filling. (Check your manufacturer's instructions for filling your water heater tank to the appropriate level.)
- When the tank is filled, turn on the water heater and you are ready to go!
- If you are storing your RV for the winter, remember to drain the water heater tank and water lines to prevent freezing. Check your RV documentation for any special details about the winterizing procedure for your unit.

- When you take the RV out of storage, remember to de-winterize the water system. Flush the antifreeze from the system. Then fill the water heater with fresh water before igniting.
- For either standard or tankless water heaters, ask a service professional to give it a check-up at least once a year. ** *Make a note for maintenance (RVMS)*

The Toilet

The standard RV toilet is basically a "drop flush", but there are also electronic models, and even composting toilets. Except for composting toilets, which carry the waste within the base of the toilet, both electronic and drop-flush toilets empty waste into the black holding tank.

Monitor the tank level to determine when to empty the black tank at a designated dump station. You will find a black tank monitor in the RV systems monitor panel. Do not dump gray or black tanks on the ground.

The Sinks and Showers

The sinks and showers draw fresh water from either the campground water hook up or, when boondocking, from the fresh water holding tank. When the fresh holding tank water is used you must switch on the water pump and wait a few moments while the pump primes before using the water. Waste water from sinks and showers empty into the gray water holding tank.

Plumbing Reminders

- Sinks and showers empty into the gray tanks. The toilet and sometimes the bathroom sink, empty into the black tank.

- If you choose a composting toilet, you will have to empty the holding chamber manually.

- Monitor the levels of fresh water, black and gray tanks on the systems monitoring panel and empty when they are full or at the end of your trip (whichever comes first!)

- Hot water for an RV is provided by either a propane/electric fueled standard six-gallon water heater or a tankless water heater fueled by either propane or electricity.

- Remember, your gray tank capacity will limit the length of your shower as much as your water heater's capacity.

The Service Bay

Truly the "business" end of the RV plumbing system, the service bay is used on every trip. You will hook up your fresh water supply and empty the gray and black tanks from the control panel inside the service bay.

Service Bay Tips:

- Keep paper towels, latex gloves and hand sanitizer in the service bay and use them every time you access the tank dump functions.

- There is "city" water and "on board" water. You hook up to city water when you are at camp. You use your on-board water when "boondocking".
- Fill the fresh water tank from a faucet or from a container. Some RVs have a direct hose connection to fill the fresh water tank, others require you to turn a valve after connecting a hose. If you're using a container instead of a hose, you'll need to use a siphon. Remember to fill the fresh water tank before you go boondocking!
- If using city water, attach a water filter to your water hose when hooking up to a campground water faucet.
- Attach a water pressure regulator to the campground faucet to monitor and adjust the pressure of the city water supply to prevent damage to your RV's plumbing system.

Emptying the Gray and Black Holding Tanks

Procedure for a standard, three Inch hose dump set-up:

Put on your latex gloves. Hook up the RV dump hose to the outlet (make sure it is secure!) and then put the other end in the dump station port. Sometimes there is a hinged port lid, sometimes there is not. If there is a hinged lid it can help keep the hose in place. For the dump station ports that don't have a hinged lid, you will often see a large rock next to the port for the same purpose (no kidding!). Make sure to keep an eye on the dump hose to make sure it stays in the dump station port.

Pull the black holding tank valve first. When it is empty, close the black tank valve and open the gray tank valve (the gray water helps rinse out the hose). Note: do not use force to open or close the valves. There is typically just a little "travel" in the valve handle.

When the tanks are empty, rinse out your dump hose (there is usually a hose for this use at most dump stations) while it is still attached to the ground dump port. Use the provided dump station hose to rinse your RV dump hose so the residue ends up in the dump station and not on the ground!

Procedure for a macerator hose set-up:

Put on your latex gloves. If you have a macerator with a cap, be sure to remove the small cap before putting it into the dump station port.

Put the macerator hose end into the dump station port, making sure it is securely in place.

IMPORTANT: make sure the hose is securely in place in the dump station port before continuing.

Pull the black tank valve and turn on the macerator. When the black tank is empty (you can see this on the tank monitor panel), turn off the pump and close the black tank valve. Note: Do not use force when opening or closing the valves. There is typically just a little "travel" in the valve handle.

Pull the gray tank valve and turn on the macerator. When the gray tank is empty, turn off the pump and close the gray tank valve. Note: Do not use force when opening or closing the valves. There is typically just a little "travel" in the valve handle.

Although you won't rinse the macerator hose with an external hose, make sure you lift the hose to help drain the last of the gray water into the dump station drain and then replace the cap onto the macerator hose to prevent any remaining fluid from leaking out.

Add a couple of gallons of fresh water and a deodorizer packet to the black tank by pouring it down the RV toilet. That means putting water back into the tank after you have emptied it. (Trust me on this one!)

You can also pour a gallon or two of fresh water into the gray tank through the kitchen sink drain along with a squirt of dish soap to help clean the tank. Adding a bit of water to the black and gray tanks after dumping helps to prevent residue from adhering to the tank walls.

Flush the holding tanks after each trip to keep them clean and reduce buildup on the tank sensors. (most RVs are equipped with a tank flush function)

How to Sanitize an RV Plumbing System

This is a general guideline, please check your RV's documentation for procedures specific to your model RV

Determine the amount of household bleach needed to sanitize the fresh water holding tank.

Multiply the capacity of the tank in gallons by 0.13 to get the number of ounces of bleach needed to sanitize the tank. For example: for a fresh water tank capacity of 24 gallons x .013 = 3.12 ounces of bleach needed.

Then mix the bleach with water in a container and add it to the fresh water tank using a syphon. Most RVs are set-up to use a syphon for this procedure (and for winterizing). If yours does not have a syphon set up, refer to your RVs documentation on adding fluids from a container.

Fill the fresh water tank with fresh water. Then open all the faucets (hot and cold) and run until you can smell the chlorine odor.

Turn off all the faucets and Let the solution soak in the tank at least four hours.

Drain the tank and refill with fresh water to flush the system until all of the chlorine odor is gone. It may require a couple of refills. There may still be a light chlorine odor or taste.

How to Winterize an RV Plumbing System

This is a general guideline, please check your RV's documentation for procedures specific to your model RV

Water left in the RV's plumbing can freeze in cold weather causing serious damage to the lines, the water pump and water heater. You must drain the whole plumbing system. Always check your manufacturer's recommendations for winterizing procedures as each RV is unique.

IMPORTANT: Use only non-toxic RV antifreeze for winterizing your RV plumbing system. It is safe for water pumps. DO NOT USE AUTOMOTIVE ANTIFREEZE! It is toxic and small amounts left in the water system can poison!

Make sure the water heater is turned off and cool. Turn the LP gas switch to "off".

Check your service bay for a "winterize" switch for the plumbing system and turn it to "winterize".

Turn the water heater to "winterize" mode. Drain the hot water tank.

Make sure your RV is not connected to a city water source.

Empty the fresh water tank.

Turn on the water pump and open up all the faucets.

Let the water pump empty the tank.

Turn off the water pump and all the faucets.

Using non-toxic RV antifreeze, syphon the non-toxic antifreeze into the fresh water system by turning on the water pump. (See your RV documentation for the amount of RV antifreeze needed for your system and any unique procedures.)

Run the faucets and shower until the pink RV antifreeze flows from the faucets instead of water. Turn off faucets and shower as soon as you see the pink antifreeze.

Flush toilet until you see pink RV antifreeze instead of water. If toilet has a separate sprayer, spray it until the pink antifreeze runs instead of water.

Turn off water pump.

Pour RV antifreeze in each drain (sinks, shower, toilet) to keep the seals and trap from freezing.

Drain the black and gray tanks at a dump station.

Open faucets to release air pressure.

Check the city water connection inlet for residual water. Depress the center stem to drain any water in the inlet. (you may have to remove a screen to access the center stem. Replace the screen when no more water drains.)

The Small-RV HVAC System

A Ninja Adapts to the Seasons

Traveling year-round enjoying eternal springtime is what most small-RV ninjas love to do. And that means knowing how to cool off or warm up the RV. That is what the HVAC system is designed to do. Although most small RVs are not designed for extreme weather, they are well equipped for temperatures from sweaters to bathing suits.

HVAC System Components List

Furnace

**Make a note of model, make, and filter size (RVIN) set maintenance schedule (RVMS)

Air Conditioner

**Make a note of model, make, and filter sizes (RVIN) set maintenance schedule (RVMS)

Thermostat

**Make a note of model, make, and filter sizes (RVIN)

LP (propane) tank

**Make a note of the size, model, and make (RVIN) set maintenance schedule (RVMSs

Ventilation fans

**Make a note of model, make, and filter sizes (RVIN) set maintenance schedule (RVMS)

How the HVAC system works

Most RVs are not four-season vehicles and are really built for warm and mild weather. If you plan on camping often in very hot or very cold areas, look into thermal window coverings. You might also check with your manufacturer about the availability and recommendations for additional insulation, holding tank heaters and plumbing wraps.

Small RVs in the class we are targeting, have a furnace and an air conditioner. They may also have a heat pump that is part of the air conditioner system. All three are usually controlled by one thermostat. The furnace runs on propane and electricity and the air conditioner and heat pump run only on shore power or the generator.

Just like at home, you turn the thermostat to heat or air conditioning and set or adjust the temperature.

Furnace and Heat Pump

While the heat pump can take the chill out of the RV, the furnace actually heats up the RV interior. The furnace uses both the propane and electricity to operate the burners, the fans, and the thermostat. The propane fuels the furnace burners to heat the air while the electricity powers the fans which move the heated air through the RV. You turn on the heat at a thermostat and the thermostat signals the propane burners to light and the fans to start.

All of this works perfectly when you are connected to shore power. If you are running on 12-volt battery power, your heat will only last as long as your battery can keep the fans running.

If you are camping in particularly cold weather and connected to shore power, a portable electric heater will help warm up the RV quicker. Use only according to the manufacturer's instructions and don't leave an electric heater unattended!

Furnace Tips:

- Service your RV furnace at least once each year. **Make a note in the maintenance schedule (RVMS)*

- Change the filters and return filters. **Make a note in the maintenance schedule (RVMS)*

- Make sure your LP tank is full when camping in cold weather.

- In cold weather, you may want to invest in thermal window coverings and use an electric heater to supplement the furnace.

- Use a heavy curtain panel between the RV cab and the coach area to insulate the coach from the cab. In cold weather, it will minimize heat loss through the windshield and side windows. In very hot weather it will create a barrier for heat coming through the windshield.

Air Conditioner

Mounted on the roof of the RV, the air conditioner can be a bit noisy inside the RV but they do a reasonable job of cooling a small RV. You can minimize the load on the air conditioner by using thermal shades or curtains on the windshield and side windows to block the sun. A small fan will help circulate the cool air and make you feel cooler - even if it doesn't drop the actual temperature!

If you are staying in very hot climates, consider a heavy curtain between the RV cab and the coach area. The curtain can block much of the heat that filters through the windshield and side windows. You might also want to put out your awning to shade the side of the RV and reduce heat impact on the interior.

Air Conditioner Tips:

- They need to be serviced every year to stay in good running condition.

**Make a note in the maintenance schedule (RVMS)*

- Keep the intake vents clean and free of debris
- Clean and/or change the return filters

**Make a note in the maintenance schedule (RVMS)*

Ventilator Fans

Fans for ventilating the coach are perfect for cooling down the RV in mild weather, removing cooking odors, and reducing dampness from the shower area. These little life-savers are workhorses. The fans can run on either shore power or battery power when boondocking.

Some units have rain sensors built-in and will close automatically when it is wet outdoors. This same feature can shut them off if there is too much steam from your shower! It's a good idea to turn on the fan before you run a shower to help ventilate the moisture more effectively.

Ventilator Fan Tips:

- Open a window furthest away from the fan for optimal air flow through the RV.
- If the screens covering the fans are dirty, carefully remove them and wash in mild soapy water, rinse well, dry, and replace.
- Check with the manufacturer on service frequency and any special recommendations on cleaners and lubricants.

**Make a note in the maintenance schedule (RVMS)

- If you have "Fantastic Fans" (that's not a judgment call - it's a brand name), some of them have an auto-close feature that turn them off and close the lid automatically when it starts to rain. You can adjust the sensor a little, but they will still close when it rains.
- Most of the power fans have a small fuse that may need to be replaced if the fan fails to operate. Add it to your maintenance schedule.

**Make a note in the maintenance schedule (RVMS)

The Engine and Chassis

A Ninja is All About Performance

As a small-RV ninja you'll find yourself drawing on all of your skills to keep your ride in razor-sharp cruising condition. From the engine to the exterior of the coach, there are a host of regular maintenance chores. Make sure you fill out the RV Maintenance Schedule to keep track of every task.

The information we offer is a general guideline. Please review your RVs documentation before doing anything we suggest. Each RV is slightly different and the manufacturers recommendations keep your warranty in force.

Engine and Chassis Components List

Chassis

** *Make a note of the VIN, the make and model of your RV (RVIN)*

Engine

** *Make a note of the fuel type, size and model of engine (RVIN)*

Fluids

** *Make a note of the oil, DEF, transmission, and coolant types your engine uses (RVIN)*

Windshield Wipers

** Make a note of the size and type (RVIN)

Automatic Leveling System

** Make a note of the model number and make (RVIN)

Tires

** Make a note of the number, type, and size tires for your RV as well as the manufacture date stamped on the tire (RVIN)

Tire Pressure Monitoring System (optional)

** Make and model (RVIN) and ** service interval (RVMS)

Back Up Camera

** Make a note of the model and make (RVIN)

Headlights

** Make a note of the model and make (RVIN)

Fuses for the Cab

** Make a note of the types, sizes and number of fuses (RVIN)

The combination of the chassis and engine is what we first recognize about an RV. We choose a style and a specific size as well as an engine type to fit our budget and how we will use our RV. For our purposes, we are considering smaller RVs and just a couple of the most common chassis types.

Chassis and Engine Combinations

Most of these Class B+ and small Class C RVs are built on a cut-away chassis. The truck manufacturer delivers the finished cab with nothing but the bare chassis structure behind it. From there, the RV manufacturer builds the coach component onto the bare chassis.

The two dominant players in this chassis size are the Mercedes-Benz Sprinter and the Ford Transit. Chrysler also makes a chassis for this type of small RV.

Gas or Diesel?

The kind of traveling you will be doing in your RV helps you decide the between engine types: gas or diesel. Most small RVs come in both gasoline or diesel engines, though the models may differ slightly. Which you choose is a matter of preference and the way you intend to use your RV.

Traditionally, diesel engines have been known for more power and torque. This helps with steep inclines and with towing a vehicle.

The down side of diesel is being very mindful of regular maintenance and keeping up with fuel quality. Even though newer RV diesel engines use an ultra-low sulfur diesel, you will still need to add DEF (Diesel Exhaust Fluid), a fuel additive to reduce emissions. Diesel engines have a long life and, if properly maintained, have fewer issues.

The benefit of a gasoline engine RV, is that it's typically less expensive than a diesel RV. The fuel economy is not as good as a diesel engine but good fuel is more readily available. On the other hand, you may not get the same level of torque/power for towing or climbing those mountain inclines. A gasoline engine is simpler to work on and service centers are easy to find. That isn't always the case with diesels.

Actual performance is unique to each brand and model. How well either a gas or a diesel engine works is also impacted by what is added to the chassis. Overall weight affects performance. If you are shopping for an RV, compare the chassis and engine specifications to get a better idea of which will best suit your intended use.

Tips for Maintaining Your RV Engine and Chassis

Note: Check your manufacturer's recommendations on engine maintenance. Since most newer engines are more complex, maintenance is best left to the pros.

- Make sure to follow the manufacturer's recommended maintenance schedule to keep your warranty in force. You can, of course, keep an eye on how the engine is running and monitor the fluid levels in your RV's engine.

** Make a note for each of the following items on your RV Maintenance Schedule (RVMS):

- Note the warranty maintenance tasks on your schedule.
- Schedule regular oil changes and add oil when needed (check manufacturer's recommended schedule).
- Monitor the oil filter and change it frequently since dirty oil can damage an engine.

- Don't forget to check on the coolant level to keep your rig running smoothly in all kinds of weather.
- Take note of the levels for the brake fluid and transmission fluid as well (some engines do not have transmission dip sticks and will have to be monitored by your service professional.)
- For diesel engines, you'll need to keep an eye on the DEF level and keep a bottle on hand to top off when needed. The RV will not use much DEF so it is easy to forget to check it. But, if you run out, you may not be able to start the RV!
- Keep the air filters clean and change when needed.
- Watch for rodents in the engine bay (they love quiet engine bays, so if yours is sitting for a while, always check for signs of nest-building!)

The Coach Body

The RV coach itself can be framed in aluminum, steel, or wood. The sheathing may be aluminum or fiberglass. Insulation for the walls and ceiling is typically polystyrene or fiberglass.

The walls and floors can be assembled in a couple of different ways:

In the "built-up" process, an interior wall surface and frame is built, then joined to the floor. Insulation, wiring, and the exterior skin are added. The wall is built in place on the chassis.

In a "laminated" process, the exterior skin, framing, insulation, and interior surface of a wall are built as a single unit and fused together before assembling with other components. In this process the wall is built and then added to the chassis.

Both methods produce a good end product and each manufacturer has their own build preferences. Though laminated builds may result in fewer "rattles", an RV is basically a rolling earthquake, so a bit of rattling seems to come with the territory.

The exterior skin of the coach is either aluminum or fiberglass and is painted. The graphics, so characteristic of RVs, can be painted on or added as something like a decal. Some fiberglass exteriors can even have graphics embedded into the fiberglass. RV roofs are made of either fiberglass, aluminum, or a rubberized material.

Regardless of the type of finish on your RV, plan on spending some time every month maintaining the exterior finish. Cleaning off road grime and insects will help preserve the RV's finish.

** *Add cleaning to your RV Maintenance Schedule (RVMS)*

Tips for Maintaining Your RV's Exterior:

- Wash your RV frequently to prevent the build-up of road grime, bugs, and stains.
- Use a mild soap compatible with the surface finish of your RV.
- Wet the surface before you apply soap, and use a soft brush or glove sponge to work the soap around the surface.
- Begin at the top and work down the side of the RV.

- IMPORTANT: When rinsing, be take care to avoid spraying water in the vents for the water heater, furnace, refrigerator, etc.
- Dead bugs on the RV's surface are hard to remove, so clean them off as soon as possible.
- Wax or polish your RV to protect its surface. Use a wax or polish that is compatible with the surface finish of your RV and always follow the manufacturers recommendations.
- Be careful when applying wax around graphics to avoid "lifting" a graphic or fading its colors.
- The surface of the RV roof may be different than the sides of the coach body. Check with the manufacture for care instructions and product recommendations.
- If you must store your RV outdoors, it will eventually show signs of UV damage. A good quality RV cover may be an option if you don't have a garage.

Small-RV Leveling Systems

A Ninja is Always Steady

A firm footing. That's what a small-RV ninja strives for at every campsite. Leveling the RV is not the most complicated task, but it is an important one. A level RV helps to ensure that appliances work properly and that you don't need safety ropes when you sleep!

Leveling Components List

Automatic-leveling-system

**Make a note of the model and make (RVIN) and the recommended service and maintenance (RVMS)

- Jack pads
- Wheel chocks

Manual leveling system

- Carpenter's level or leveling app
- Wheel chocks
- Leveling blocks

How leveling your RV works

Do you ever wonder why leveling the RV is important? Aside from the discomfort factor of camping on an angle, leveling the RV is important to the operation of your RV systems. For instance, the LP (propane) fuel used by the refrigerator, water heater, and cook top need a free and continuous flow to work properly. When the RV is not level, the flow to these appliances can be compromised.

Leveling is also important if you have a slide room. The RV has to be level for the mechanism in the slide to work properly. If the RV is not level, the slide mechanism can bind up making it difficult to put the slide out or bring it back in.

The process of manually leveling the RV can take a bit of practice but it is not difficult. If you have an automatic leveling system installed, then the leveling operation is more or less done for you at the press of a button.

Automatic Levelers

As convenient as an automatic leveling system is, there is one disadvantage: the extra weight. The added weight of the leveling system will impact your fuel mileage, and the increased gross vehicle weight, in turn, reduces how much you can safely carry in your RV. *(See the section on Gross Vehicle Weight)*

Nonetheless, the process for leveling with an automatic system couldn't be easier. Find the most level spot on the campsite, put jack pads down under where the leveling "feet" will fall, and hit the level button on your RV. You'll hear a bit of noise as the leveling feet deploy and the unit will rise and fall a bit as it finds level. Done!

Tips for Automatic Leveling Systems

- Weight: Make sure you find out if your automatic levelers are included in the GVWR. If they are an aftermarket accessory, the additional weight will limit your cargo capacity.
- Servicing: Follow the manufacturer's recommendation on servicing and adjusting automatic leveling systems.
- Jack Pads: Buy "jack pads" for each of the automatic leveling "feet". Put them on the ground under each leveling point to provide an even surface for the levelers. These pads also prevent levelers from damaging pavement and can help reduce sinking into soft surfaces.
- Chock the Wheels: Remember to chock one of the wheels to prevent the RV from rolling.

Manual Leveling

Manual leveling is not difficult but it can be frustrating until you get the hang of it. First you need to determine what part of the RV is too low. You can gauge the level of the RV with a simple carpenter's level or use a phone app for this purpose.

Then you will add leveling bricks or blocks (the ones we use look like big Lego bricks) in front of the tires on the side (and/or end) of the RV that is sitting too low. Roll up onto the bricks and recheck for level. You may need a few tries before you get it "just right" but you will get better at this with experience.

Tips for Manual Leveling with Blocks or Bricks

- Brick Style: If you have to use manual leveling bricks, we have found the "Lego-style" to be the easiest and least expensive option.
- Finding Level: To use manual leveling bricks, determine which side is out of level (side to side and front to back). We have used a smart phone app by Truma and also have used a carpenter's level. Both options work well.
- Using Bricks: Begin by setting up the leveling bricks under the front of the tire that needs to be adjusted. You may find both front tires need height or just one side, or one side front and back.
- Roll up onto the brick and re-check the level. If you need to add bricks, use two as a platform and a third attached to both platform bricks as the "step up".
- If you need still more height, add a third platform brick, use two second level bricks that snap into place holding the three platform bricks together, and then add one more brick as the next "step up". You are building a platform and staircase for the RV to roll up onto.
- If you need more bricks, maybe it's time to find a more level area!
- Chock the Wheels: Remember to chock one of the wheels to keep the RV from rolling after it is leveled.

Your RV's Tires

A Ninja Has a Solid Foundation

There is a lot riding on your tires – literally! As a novice ninja you have reached one of the most important parts of your training. The tires of your RV determine both your comfort and safety on the road.

Most small RVs have either four or six tires depending on the chassis and weight of the coach. Dual tires on the rear of the coach help provide stability and handling.

Driving miles typically dictate when tires should be rotated, aligned, balanced, and replaced. But you may be surprised to learn, that when tires are not used, there is still a need to replace them. Dry rot is a common ailment with RV tires when an RV is stored for months on end without moving or is stored outdoors where the UV rays can break down the tire.

Additionally, the correct tire pressure is as critical for extending tire life as it is for safe driving. Get a good quality tire pressure gauge and use it often! Check your vehicle's documentation for recommended tire pressures for different environmental conditions and different loads.

There are tire pressure monitoring systems on the market to help keep track of the RV's tire pressure. This is especially helpful with dual wheels, since it is more difficult to check those pressures manually. Your RV dealer may offer a tire pressure monitoring system as an option or you may purchase them as aftermarket accessories. Check the reviews from RV owners as well as online forums to help you choose the system that is right for your RV.

Tips for Maintaining Your Tires

- **Tire Pressure:** Check tire pressure regularly. This is especially important before and during a trip. Even if you have an automatic pressure monitor, it's a good habit to check the tire pressure manually once in a while.

- **Dual Wheels:** If your RV has dual wheels make sure you check the tire pressure on the inside tire as well as the outside tire. It can be a bit inconvenient and it would seem that valve extensions might be an answer, but valve extensions tend to leak. If you choose to install them, be vigilant about checking the tire pressure.

- **Tire Wear:** Check your RV's tires for wear and have them rotated on a regular basis to distribute the wear pattern.

**Make a note in the maintenance schedule (RVMS)

- **Keep Tires Balanced:** Make sure to have the tires aligned and balanced before each trip.

**Make a note in the maintenance schedule (RVMS)

- **Replacing Tires:** Replace tires when they show wear. You might also note down the manufacture date stamped on the tire. Some sources tell us that tires should be replaced every 5-7 years regardless of wear since dry rot could set it. When your tires are nearing their end-of-life, don't wait – replace them. There's nothing like sitting on the side of the road with a flat during vacation! Make sure you get the proper size and type of tire when you replace them.

**Make a note of the model and size in your notebook (RVIN)

Additional Equipment Items

A Ninja Loves a Little Bling

Just because ninjas dress in black does not mean they don't appreciate a few accessories. Not all small RVs have the following items. If yours does, by all means include it in your notebook.

Automatic Step - ***Make a note of the model and make (RVIN) Note servicing and maintenance (RVMS)*

Automatic Awning - ***Make a note of the model and make (RVIN) Note servicing and maintenance (RVMS)*

Generator - ***Make a note of the model and make (RVIN) Note servicing and maintenance (RVMS)*

Macerator - ***Make a note of the model and make (RVIN) Note servicing and maintenance (RVMS)*

Refrigerator/Freezer - ***Make a note of the model and make (RVIN) Note servicing and maintenance (RVMS)*

Stove - ***Make a note of the model and make (RVIN) Note servicing and maintenance (RVMS)*

Microwave - **Make a note of the model and make (RVIN) Note servicing and maintenance (RVMS)*

Automatic Retracting Steps

Many newer RVs have automatic retracting steps at the coach door. When the engine is started, or the door is closed, the steps retract under the coach body. When the door is opened, the steps extend to allow easier access to the coach. There is usually a switch inside the RV to keep the steps in the extended position while in camp.

In some units the automatic steps are linked to a magnet in the door frame. If the door or door lock has become loose, the steps may not function because the magnets don't line up. (Try tightening up the door lock screws.)

When the engine starts, the steps automatically retract in most models.

Lubricate the step mechanism every month – even when you are not camping.

Automatic Awning

Protecting you from too much sun or a little bit of rain, the awning makes camping more enjoyable. There are several types: freestanding, leg supports, and supports on the coach body. If your awing has supports make sure to use them to prevent the awning from sagging or tearing.

Awning Tips

- Lubricate the mechanism frequently. The sun and wind can bake the mechanical unit.

- If it is windy, close the awning. A ripped awning is an expensive fix.
- Most awnings have legs. If yours does, use them. Either secured into brackets on the RV or standing on the ground they give support to the awning. Some newer awnings do not have legs.
- Brush debris from the awning before retracting.
- If it gets wet, let the awning dry completely before retracting it to prevent mold.
- Clean the awning fabric according to manufacturer's recommendations.

The RV Kitchen

A Ninja Has to Eat

A true small-RV ninja actually uses the RV kitchen. Cooking on the road is a great way to "taste" a destination, shopping local farmer's markets or fishing piers. If that weren't enough, it may help you to stay on budget!

The kitchen is a system unto itself. With at least three major appliances - and multitude of accessory appliances, it functions well on shore power, generator power, LP, and even battery power.

The Refrigerator/Freezer

Most RV refrigerators run on three types of power: electricity from shore power, electricity from the coach batteries, and propane. Most of the newer models are automatic and will switch to the best appropriate power source without your intervention.

RV refrigerators are not as efficient at cooling down food as they are at keeping it cool. So, if you put warm food or beverages in the refrigerator, they will raise the temperature of the whole unit and it may take a long time to recover. It is best to put only cold foods and drinks in the fridge.

RV Refrigerator Tips

- Leave lots of air circulation room in your fridge. If the air doesn't circulate, the fridge doesn't cool.
- The freezer works pretty well if you pack it lightly and load only frozen food. Air circulation is a key.
- Consider taking a small cooler with ice for canned and bottled drinks. The easier access will keep you from opening the fridge too often!

The Stove Cooktop

Although there are some electric models, most RV stoves are propane powered and work much like a gas stove at home. They typically have a push button igniter to make lighting the burners easier.

Propane Stove Tips

- Check the jets periodically for clogs and have it serviced by a propane professional annually. ** Make a note on your maintenance schedule (RVMS)
- Always open a window when using the propane stove to avoid setting off the LP alarm
- Clean the stove after each use to prevent crumbs and liquids from clogging the gas jet openings.

The Microwave Oven

You may have a variety of additional appliances in your RV kitchen, the most commonly installed small appliance is the microwave oven. It needs good ventilation to cool down between uses. It's not a great idea to use them for long periods of time if its location is not well ventilated. Since they draw a lot of power, microwave ovens may not work through an inverter. They require the steady power flow of a generator or shore power.

Gross Vehicle Weight Rating

A Ninja Knows Their Capacity

Although ninjas are brave, overloading an RV is too dangerous for even an experienced ninja. It may be tempting to bring all your ninja toys along, but there is a limit for every RV.

Every RV has a Gross Vehicle Weight Rating (GVWR). The Gross Vehicle Weight Rating is the heaviest weight, determined by the manufacturer, for the safe operation of your RV.

Terminology

The **Gross Vehicle Weight** is the actual weight of the fully loaded RV including all cargo, fluids, passengers and optional equipment as well as the tongue weight of any towed vehicle (The towed vehicle and the RV have separate GVWRs).

There is also a **Gross Vehicle Axle Weight Rating**. This rating is for the maximum weight on an axle, but assumes the load is equally balanced. In these small RVs there isn't a lot of storage space to add weight too unevenly, but give weight distribution some thought when you are packing up.

The **Unloaded Vehicle Weight** (UVW) is the weight of the RV as it comes from the factory with a full tank of fuel and engine fluids. This weight does not include any potable water weight, propane, occupants, or dealer installed accessories.

How much can you bring along?

If you want to figure out how much "stuff" you can take along in your RV, you will have to determine the Gross Vehicle Weight Rating minus the following weights:

- Unloaded Vehicle Weight (UVW described above)
- A full fresh water tank (@8.3 lbs. per gallon)
- The water in the water heater (@8.3 lbs. per gallon)
- A full LP (propane) tank (@4.2 lbs. per gallon)
- The number of passengers the RV can sleep (@ 154 lbs. each)
- And any dealer-installed accessories' weight

The resulting figure is how much cargo weight you can add and stay within the GVWR.

Tips about GVWR

- Weigh your RV (first empty, and then fully loaded). You can do this at many truck-stops for a nominal fee. Most will print out how the weight is distributed on each axle.

- Your RV has a designation for the amount of weight to be carried by each axle. If the weight is unevenly distributed between axles, see if you can redistribute the weight.
- Remember to adjust the tire pressure to accommodate the load and ensure safe handling.

Towing a Car

Some Ninjas Have Toads

Ninjas usually work alone but some like to bring along a toad. It's not a companionship thing, they just want another way to get around.

Small RVs are great by themselves and many people choose a small RV so they won't have to tow a vehicle. We have found that using our RV like a car works well while traveling. If we feel it is too large for a crowded downtown area, we simply rent a car at that destination or use a service like "Uber".

Nonetheless, some people just want to take along a car. There are so many variables for towing a vehicle that we cannot make specific recommendations but we can offer some basic information.

Choosing a Toad

You will need to check your RV's documentation to see how heavy a vehicle can be towed. Then, you'll need to determine if you have – or have to buy – a towable vehicle. Not all cars can be towed "four wheels down" and doing so when a car is not designed for towing, can result in major damage to its drive train.

The type of towing will also have to be considered. Using a tow bar, a dolly or a trailer are the choices to evaluate. Some insurers prefer one method over another so it pays to check with your insurance company before settling on a tow vehicle and tow method.

There is also some additional expense to consider with towing. Apart from the equipment for towing you'll need to consider the added weight of the towing components, impact on fuel mileage and the wear and tear on your RV.

Components for towing a car

"Four Wheels Down" towing

Ball couple or swivel mount: One of these will attach to the RV and, in turn, a tow bar.

Tow bar: The connection between the RV and the tow vehicle.

Hitch receiver: Bolted or welded to the frame of the tow vehicle to receive the tow bar.

Wiring harness and safety cable: Connects brakes and lights from the RV to the towed vehicle and the safety cable hold onto the vehicle in the event it becomes "unhitched".

Auxiliary Braking system for the vehicle being towed

Dolly or Trailer towing

Ball couple

Trailer or dolly (Note: small RVs may not be able to accommodate the weight of a car trailer)

Straps to secure car to dolly or trailer

Wiring harness and safety cables or chains.

For towing, you will need to know the Gross Combination Weight Rating (GCWR) which is the total weight allowed for the RV and the towed vehicle combined. This figure includes the weight of the hitch and any towing accessories for the car.

In your RV documentation, the manufacturer may list a maximum vehicle weight the RV can safely tow. If that weight is not specified you can figure it out by subtracting the GVWR from the GCWR. The difference is the weight you can tow. And, no, you can't load up the car with stuff unless you add that weight to the equation and the total is within the GCWR!

Be sure to find the right size and hitch rating for what you are towing. Consider the towing capacity of the RV as well as the ratings of the tow bar, the cables, the base plates and connector. Actual towing capacity is determined by the lowest rating of any one part in the "chain" of towing parts.

Tips for Towing a Vehicle

- If you decide to tow a car, research which type of car is best for your RV and your use. Choose the lightest vehicle that will fit your needs and stay within the Gross Combination Weight Rating.

- Check with your insurance company before selecting a "toad" vehicle and the method to tow it.

- Install a secondary braking system for the car that works with your RVs braking system. Since RVs are difficult to stop, adding a car to that equation makes a second braking system necessary.

- If you are towing a vehicle, make a point to do a "360" tour around your whole rig before you leave and every time you make a stop. Inspect the connections, brakes, and lights.

A Few Tips for Using Your RV

A Ninja Knows All the Secrets

You are nearing the end of your small-RV ninja training so it's time to reveal a few secrets about small RVs. From driving and parking tips to learning how to troubleshoot problems, a certified small-RV ninja must adopt the mantra of "I am ready for anything!"

Driving a Small RV

Many people purchase small RVs for their maneuverability - they are easy to drive and park. That said, they are probably larger than most family-sized vehicles like trucks, SUVs or mini-vans. The tendency, though, is to drive them like the family car - but you can't.

The length, height, and weight of a small RV changes the way it handles from what you might be accustomed to. You can't just "jump in and go". It takes a little practice to understand a few key elements about your small RV.

First, it's height. Find out the exact height of your RV including the air conditioner unit and antennae. Most RVs in this class stand tall at about 10 - 11 feet. That's higher than some bridges and overpasses in older communities.

It was a little unsettling when we found so many older bridges without any height marking! So how do you know if your RV will fit? Consider a few options: Watch to see it there are tall tractor-trailers and buses going under the bridge. If there is little traffic, you could measure the bridge. Or, if that isn't practical, just turn around and find a different route.

This is why choosing a route for your trip is important. Check with RV route planners and detailed truck maps to avoid low bridges. There are GPS devices specially made for RVs that can help you with bridge heights by steering you around low bridges.

Second, the weight of your RV is substantial. Unlike a car, your RVs gross weight makes it less maneuverable. It takes a long time to come to a stop and it leans heavy into curves. Take your time, slow down, and get the feel of your RV's weight. Take corners wider and slower than you would in an SUV or truck.

Plan on more distance between you and other vehicles on the road - there is no "quick stop" in an RV! If you do slam on the brakes it will still take a long distance to bring the unit to a stop - and you will find anything not secured in the back rolling to the front!

Another caution regarding your RV's weight is for bridges. Most bridges post a maximum load they can safely carry. Make sure the bridges you cross can hold the weight of your RV. You can have your fully-loaded RV weighed at many truck stops. It doesn't cost much and it is a good thing to know!

The third consideration, is the length of your RV. Most small RVs come in between 24-32 feet in length - considerably longer than most family vehicles. That means making turns requires using those side mirrors to make sure you clear the curb!

Driving a small RV is much easier than handling a larger one. But there will still be a few adjustments to your driving habits before you can feel confident piloting your small RV. While you're thinking about it, make a note of the height, length, and gross weight of your RV and tape it to driver's side sun visor. That way, if you need to know, the information is right there in front of you.

RV Driving Tips

- Always do a "360" walk and check around the exterior of your unit before driving. Close and secure all doors, compartments, and anything attached to the vehicle. (i.e., bike racks, etc.)
- Clean and adjust side mirrors. Learn to use them and trust them.
- This is a heavy vehicle. It does not stop on a dime. Stay well behind the car in front of you and be vigilant about traffic around you.
- An RV needs extra room for turns. You will probably take up a full lane to make a turn. Embrace it.
- An RV does not "scratch out". Wait for a reasonable opening before pulling out. Remember, you are carrying a vacation cabin in the back seat.

Parking

Its small size is a huge benefit! Most small RVs will fit into a single parking space width-wise but may need a little extra length. Get accustomed to backing into a parking space. It is so much easier to back in knowing your blocking traffic than trying to back out not knowing what's behind you!

RV Parking Tips:

- How much space your RV requires depends on its length and width. Most Class B+ and some Class C units are about 25 feet in length and about 8 feet in width. That is narrow enough for a parking space but longer than most parking spaces.
- Practice backing into a parking space. It will make parking easier in the long run.
- If you back into a parking space bordered by a sidewalk, you may be able to overhang the sidewalk and almost fit into the space if you bring the back tires right to the curb.
- Make it easy on yourself. If there is room to park "broadside" that is the ultimate!

Troubleshooting problems with your RV

No matter what brand or model RV you purchase, there will always be problems that arise. Keep in mind that you are traveling down the road with a house in the back seat. The constant movement is going to shake things loose. Add to that, the simple wear and tear of using the RV results in things wearing out or breaking – just like things at home.

When something doesn't work the way it should, it's time for a little sleuthing to figure out what's gone wrong. Start with the simplest fix first. You'd be surprised at how many "problems" are just operator error! A quick look at the basics like how things are set up, plugged in (or not), switched on, having enough power or fuel to run a component are the first steps in troubleshooting.

Once you determine the unit is properly set up, plugged in, turned on, and has adequate power, fuel, or water then it's time to review the offending system's components. You may be able to narrow down which component is not working by testing each one in the operational chain - from where the system begins to where the problem occurs.

Once you narrow down the "suspects" you'll need to determine if the problem is something you can fix yourself or if you need to find professional help.

For instance, when we had no electricity, we started our troubleshooting where we discovered the problem – at the outlets. We first checked to see if any

GFCIs were tripped. Then the fuse panel got a quick inspection before moving on to check that the battery bank was turned to the "on" position.

Then we checked the battery charge level. The next step was to check the inverter to see if power was moving from the battery bank to the outlets. And then, we checked to make sure the inverter was switched on, and then checked the "reset" button. For us, this took a phone call to our maintenance tech for help.

If we had been plugged into shore power, we would have checked the campground connection to make sure it was switched "on" and then checked the surge protector to make sure we had good current. The next item would have been the RV power cord. If we still didn't have power, we would have checked the battery level and inverter – and if all that didn't help, we would call for help.

We have also found that connections get loose with all the vibration of driving. So, when we're troubleshooting, we check any connections or parts that might be loose. It is as much a part of the troubleshooting process as testing the function of the components.

It is not unthinkable to find that a component has "gone bad". A quick search on the internet will turn up hundreds of entries from RVers who are struggling with failed appliances, components and parts. Some are poorly made but most seem to fail after a lot of use or inadequate maintenance. Every appliance and part have a "life-span" and will eventually need to be replaced — just like in your house.

We had a brand-new model of a refrigerator/freezer that suddenly stopped working — less than a month after we bought the RV. It didn't take long to search out the issue on the internet — the new model had a faulty "motherboard" and it was well documented on the web by many RVers.

A call to the fridge manufacturer (not the RV manufacturer) resulted in a new fridge within a week. They knew there was an issue and, to their credit, they resolved it immediately.

Something to consider is that RV manufacturers do not make the appliances. So, when an appliance fails it might make more sense to contact the appliance manufacturer for help. If your RV warranty covers such failures than by all means call the RV manufacturer.

Troubleshooting is a process of elimination and once you have exhausted all the options from set up to looking for loose connections, it's time to call for help. No shame in that! No one can know everything and we have found service techs and other RVers to be generous with sharing their experience.

Checklists

A Ninja Always Has a Plan

It's time to test all of your new small-RV ninja knowledge. Camping with the RV is a wonderful adventure and, once we choose a destination, we are always anxious to get on the road. But, before we pack up and go, there are few items to check to make sure the RV is both road-worthy and campground ready.

Pre-Trip Checklist

Scheduled Warranty Service: are you up to date?

Oil: check the level and top off if needed

Oil filter: is it time to change?

Coolant: is the right antifreeze or coolant in the radiator?

DEF: If you have a diesel engine, is the DEF level topped off?

Fuel: gotta fill the tank!

Windshield Wiper Blades: How are they holding up? Is it time for replacement blades?

Windshield Wiper Fluid: Top up the tank.

Air Filters: both the engine and cabin filters need a quick inspection.

Batteries: are all the batteries charged and holding a charge?

Tires: Check for wear, and then check the tire pressure

Brake fluid: check the level.

Lubrication: If your RV has been sitting a while, lubricate the automatic step, slide out, awning mechanism, and any other accessory that requires lubrication.

Generator: test it!

Solar Panels: clean them

Propane Tank: fill it up

Holding tanks: fill the fresh water tank; put several gallons of water in the gray and black tanks along with a deodorizer tablet. (If the RV has been in storage, this is a particularly good idea!)

Water pump: test

Water heater: test

Check to make sure these items are packed:

Leveling blocks or jack pads

Surge protector

Water pressure regulator

Fresh water hose

Shore power cord

Service bay: latex gloves, hand sanitizer, paper towels

Air Conditioner/Furnace: test

Return filters: do they need cleaning or replacing?

Cooktop: test

Refrigerator/Freezer: test

Wash and wax exterior of RV

Clean interior of RV including cooktop, refrigerator/freezer, and bathroom fixtures

Make your packing list!

We have provided two sets of camp checklists: one for camping with electricity and water hook-ups and the other set for boondocking without any electricity or water hook-ups.

Setting Up Camp Checklist (standard hook-ups)

Check-in to campground and find campsite. Put up the "reserved" card on the site post if required.

Inspect the site for the most level spot

Level the RV with either the automatic levelers or with the manual blocks or bricks

Make sure inverter, generator, water heater, and water pump are in the "off" position when hooking up to campground supply.

Test the campground electricity before hooking up; if ok, hook up surge protector and electrical cord

Test the campground water pressure with a water pressure regulator before hooking it up to the RV

Hook up the TV Cable (if any)

Once the unit is level, and the electricity is hooked up, extend the slide room (if you have one)

Put out the awning

Set up camp chairs

Observe Camp Etiquette:

- Keep music and noise to reasonable levels during the day, and adhere to quiet hours in the evening.
- If your fire is producing too much heavy smoke, put it out.
- Don't run your generator continuously, especially if you are camping with a lot of tent campers (they can't get away from the noise and fumes)
- Report any safety issues to the park ranger or campground management if you find faulty electrical or water connections, or broken campground equipment.

Breaking Down Camp (standard hook-ups)

Make sure the campfire is completely cold with no steam or smoke. Stir the ashes to be sure.

Remove all trash from the site and dispose of it in the appropriate campground trash dumpsters.

Clean your camp site, retuning table to original place if you have moved it. Remove any trash, leftover food or your own broken equipment.

Fill fresh water tank if depleted.

Retract the awning and slide room.

Turn off air conditioner or furnace

Turn off any extra appliances (i.e., coffee maker, crockpot, etc.)

Turn off and close ventilator fans

Un-hook electrical cord and surge protector, put away in storage compartment.

Un-hook water, pressure regulator and filter, put away in storage compartment.

Bring RV down from levelers or roll off the leveling blocks.

Take a quick inventory to make sure everything is where it should be in your rig.

Make sure you re-pack all of your belongings. Check the electrical cord, water hose, surge protector, water pressure regulator, water filter, leveling blocks, camp chairs and tables, wheel chocks, and leveling blocks, etc.

Secure all drawers and cabinets, sliding doors.

Close windows and secure shades

Make sure inverter, generator, and the water pump are all in the "off" position

Secure service bay

Conduct a "360" tour around your RV to make sure all storage compartment doors are closed and secured, camping gear is put away, awning and slide are pulled in (if you have them), wheel chocks and levelers put are away, water hose and electrical cord put away. Then check the tires, and just give a good look all over the RV to make sure there are no stray branches on the roof, etc.

Take RV to dump station (put on latex gloves)

Standard Dump Hose

If using a 3" dump hose, feed it into the dump station port, secure.

Pull black tank valve empty black tank. Close black tank valve.

Pull the gray tank valve and empty the gray tank. Close the gray tank valve.

Rinse 3" dump hose with water into dump station port and return the hose to its storage compartment.

Macerator Dump Hose

If using a macerator hose, uncap and feed into the dump station port, secure.

Pull the black tank valve, and then turn on the macerator.

Monitor the tank level until empty. Turn off the macerator and close the black valve.

Pull the gray tank valve and then turn on the macerator.

Monitor the tank level until empty. Turn off the macerator and close the gray tank valve.

Lift and empty macerator hose into the dump station port and then replace macerator hose cap and return to its storage compartment.

Check to make sure valves to gray and black tank are in the closed position

Turn on the water pump and fill a couple of gallon jugs with fresh water from the RV fresh water holding tank:

Pour the fresh water into the gray tank through the kitchen sink drain, with a teaspoon of dish washing liquid.

Then repeat, pouring a couple of gallons of fresh water into the black tank through the toilet. Toss in a deodorizer packet to black tank through the toilet.

Toss latex gloves and wash hands.

Take any trash to the campground dumpster.

Setting Up Camp (boondocking)

Check-in to campground and find campsite. Put up the "reserved" card on the site post (if applicable)

Try different areas of the site for the most level spot and Level the RV with either the automatic levelers or with the manual blocks or bricks (see above)

Once the unit is level, start the generator and extend the slide room (if you have one)

Check the battery charge level and run generator until charged.

Turn off generator unless cooling down unit with air conditioner. Turn off as soon as practical.

Turn on inverter and water pump

Put out the awning

Set up camp chairs

Observe Camp Etiquette:

Keep music and noise to reasonable levels during the day, and adhere to quiet hours in the evening.

If your fire is producing too much heavy smoke, put it out.

Don't run your generator continuously, especially if you are camping with a lot of tent campers (they can't get away from the noise and fumes)

Breaking Down Camp (boondocking)

Make sure the campfire is completely cold with no steam or smoke. Stir the ashes to be sure.

Remove all trash from the site and dispose of in the appropriate campground trash dumpsters.

Clean your camp site, returning table to original place if you have moved it. Remove any trash, leftover food or your own broken equipment.

Make sure you re-pack all of your belongings. Check leveling blocks, camp chairs and tables, etc. Take a quick inventory to make sure everything is where it should be in your rig.

Retract the awning and slide room.

Turn off all appliances (i.e., coffee maker, crockpot, etc.)

Secure all drawers and cabinets, sliding doors.

Close windows and secure shades

Turn off and close ventilator fans

Make sure the inverter, generator, and water pump switches are in the "off" position

Secure service bay

Conduct a "360" tour around your RV to make sure all storage compartment doors are closed and secured, camping gear is put away, awning and slide are pulled in (if you have them), wheel chocks and levelers put are away, water hose and electrical cord put away. Then check the tires, and just give a good look all over the RV to make sure there are no stray branches on the roof, etc.

Take RV to dump station, put on latex gloves

Standard Dump Hose

If using a 3" dump hose, feed it into the dump station port, secure.

Pull black tank valve empty black tank. Close black tank valve.

Pull the gray tank valve and empty the gray tank. Close the gray tank valve.

Rinse 3" dump hose with water into dump station port and return the hose to its storage compartment.

Macerator Dump Hose

If using a macerator hose, uncap and feed into the dump station port, secure.

Pull the black tank valve, and then turn on the macerator.

Monitor the tank level until empty. Turn off the macerator and close the black valve.

Pull the gray tank valve and then turn on the macerator.

Monitor the tank level until empty. Turn off the macerator and close the gray tank valve.

Lift and empty macerator hose into the dump station port and then replace macerator hose cap and return to its storage compartment.

Check to make sure valves to gray and black tank are in the closed position

Turn on the water pump and fill a couple of gallon jugs with fresh water from the RV fresh water holding tank:

Pour the fresh water into the gray tank through the kitchen sink drain, with a teaspoon of dish washing liquid.

Then repeat, pouring a couple of gallons of fresh water into the black tank through the toilet. Toss in a deodorizer packet to black tank through the toilet.

Toss latex gloves and wash hands.

Take any trash to the campground dumpster.

Toss latex gloves and wash hands.

Take any trash to the campground dumpster.

Glossary of RV and RV Camping Terms

AC/DC Electrical Current – Alternating Current and Direct Current. In an RV this refers to the AC power supplied by a generator or a shore power connecting to run appliances and systems of the RV. Direct Current is the power supplied by the RV battery bank and must be inverted to Alternating Current for use by the RV's appliances and systems.

Battery Bank – The multiple batteries used for an RV's house functions. Typically, there are at least two deep-cycle batteries connected to an inverter.

Black Tank – Holding tank for toilet waste.

Boondocking – Camping or overnighting without a hook-up for electricity or water.

City Water – Water source under pressure provided by a campground for use with RVs or campers.

Composting Toilet - A self-contained waste system using an absorbent medium rather than a typical holding tank system. The chamber within the base needs to be emptied regularly and new absorbent medium to be replenished.

Converter – A device which converts Alternating Current to Direct Current. In an RV this allows the battery bank to be charged from a generator or shore power source.

Deep Cycle Battery – Stores and supplies power for an RV's functions. It is designed to be discharged for longer periods of time without damage.

DEF – Diesel Exhaust Fluid. Additive for diesel engines that reduce emissions from the exhaust.

Dinghy – A vehicle and/or trailer towed by an RV.

Dry Camping – Camping without a hook-up for electricity or water.

Dump Station – Facility at a campground or rest stop that allows RVs to dump the gray and black holding tanks.

Fresh Water Hook-Up – Faucet at a campground which provides a fresh water source for and RV campsite.

Fresh Water Tank – Holding tank for potable water used for sink faucets, shower, and toilet flush.

Full Hook-ups – Full hook-ups include electricity, water, and sewer hook-ups for RVs.

GCWR – Gross Combined Weight Rating. This is the weight of the RV and the towed vehicle weight combined, including passengers and cargo

Generator – Diesel or LP powered power plant that supplies AC current for an RV's appliances. It can also act as a charger for the RV's battery bank when equipped with a converter.

Gray Tank – Holding tank for gray water from showers and sinks.

Gross Axle Weight – The allowable safe weight of the RV on each axel.

GVWR – Gross Vehicle Weight Rating is the safe weight for operating a vehicle that includes the weight of the vehicle, fluids, passengers, and any cargo.

Hitch – The accessory attached to the RV to accommodate towing.

Hitch receiver – The accessory attached to a trailer or a vehicle allowing it to be towed by an RV.

Holding Tanks – Three tanks under the RV to hold fresh water, gray water, and black waste.

Hook-Ups – Electricity and water facilities available at campsites for RVs.

Inverter – Electrical device that "inverts" Direct Current power from the RV batteries to Alternating Current power to the RV's power outlets and devices.

Leveling Jacks – System to level the RV when camping. Automatic systems gauge the position of each wheel and lower a "jack" to raise the lowest point(s) of the RV to a level position relative to the rest of the RV wheels and the ground.

LP – Liquid Propane. Often used as a fuel for generators, RV water heaters, cooktops, and Refrigerators.

Macerator – In an RV a device that grinds up waste from the black tank to a slurry which can be moved by pump to empty the tanks.

Pull-Through Site - A campsite which allows an RV to pull into one end and exit on the other rather than backing into a site.

Sea Shower – An "on-off" system of conservation water use. Water is turned on to wet down then turned off while soaping up. Water is turned on again to rinse.

Service Bay – Compartment on the exterior of an RV where the plumbing terminates for hook-ups to external water and dumping facilities.

Shore Power – Electrical source providing Alternating Current. For RVs, this is typically the campground shore power source and at home an electrical outlet.

Slide-Out/Slide Room – A portion of the RV wall that expands away from the body of the coach on rails or tracks to provide more interior space.

Solar Panel - Panels of photo voltaic cells that generate power from sunlight.

Standard Site – A campsite with electricity and water and, often, requires the RV to back-into the site rather than pull-through it.

Surge Protector – Accessory used at the end of an electrical cord to stop power surges from campground electrical sources from damaging an RV.

Systems Monitor Panel – Electric console that displays the status of various RV's system including the fresh water, gray and black holding tanks, battery charge level, inverter switch, generator switch and hour indicator, water pump switch, and water heater switch.

Toad – A vehicle and/or trailer towed by an RV.

Tow Bar – the accessory linking the RV to the towed vehicle.

Walk-Around 360 – A practice of checking every side of an RV before driving. It includes checking all the exterior compartments to be sure they are closed and secured, all equipment is stowed away, checking the tires, and the general condition of the RV's exterior.

Water Pressure Regulator – Accessory used on the end of a water hose to determine the pressure of water delivery from a campground or "city" water faucet.

Water Pump – Mechanical pump to move water from the fresh water holding tank to faucets, shower, and toilet.

Thank you for reading!

I hope you found this book helpful for your small-RV adventure. You are a true small-RV ninja for making it to the end!

Feedback from my readers is the best way to improve my content, so I would love to hear from you. Let me know if you would like to read more about a particular RV-related topic. Or, if you have RV questions, head over to my blog at https://www.beachnana.com and I will do my best to answer them!

In the meantime, could you leave me a review on Amazon letting me know what you thought of the book? Thank you!

All the best!

Robin

About the Author

After a twenty-five-year career in tourism, Robin and her husband Jim took a year off from work to travel in their newly purchased RV. Robin decided to document their travels in a weekly blog. When the sabbatical year was over, Jim decided to retire and Robin decided to keep writing!

Robin writes an RV-travel blog at Beach Nana Travels (www.beachnana.com) and has been a guest blogger for the Leisure Travel Vans corporate website.

She has written an additional Small-RV Ninja guide for Trip Planning as well as two books based on her experience with destinations and meeting planning (The Meeting Workshop, and The Reunion Workshop). All are available for Kindle on Amazon.com.

Your RV Information Notebook

Keeping your RV information all in one place is a good practice and this convenient notebook will help you do just that. You may want to make a copy or download a copy to print from our website at www.beachnana.com/bonus-content-srvn .

Your RV's Profile

Height of RV:	
Width of RV:	
Length of RV:	
GVWRating:	
Actual Weight:	
GCVWRating:	
Actual Weight:	
Tow Vehicle Weight:	

The Engine and Chassis Profile:

VIN#:	
Engine Type:	
RV Make and Model:	
Ignition Key Code:	
Oil Filter Size:	
Oil Type:	
DEF (Diesel only):	
Transmission Fluid & Change Frequency:	
Coolant Type:	
Cabin Air Filters:	

Engine Filters:	
Windshield Wipers:	
Tire Size and Type:	
Tire Pressure:	
Tire Pressure Monitor System Make and Model:	
Automatic Stabilizers Make and Model:	
Automatic Levelers Make and Model:	
Headlight Type:	
Fuses for Cab and Engine:	

The Coach Electrical System

Coach batteries - Number and Type:	
Propane Tank Size:	
Generator Make and Model:	
Solar Panels – Number, Make and Model:	
Inverter Size, Make and Model:	
Outlets – Location of Interior Outlets:	

Location of Inverter outlets:	
Location of Exterior Outlets:	
Monitor Panel Make and Model:	
Location of Interior Fuse Panel:	
Location of GFCI Outlets:	
Surge Protector Make and Model:	

The Coach Plumbing System

Water Heater Type, Make and Model:	
Water Pump Make and Model:	
Water Filter Size, Make, Model:	
Toilet Make and Model:	
Water Pressure Regulator Make and Model:	
Macerator Make and Model:	
Macerator Hose Make and Model:	

Automatic Holding Tank Flush Make and Model:	
Holding Tank Capacities (Fresh/Gray/Black):	
Service Bay Location:	
NOTES:	

Appliance Information

Refrigerator/Freezer Make and Model:	
Cooktop Type, Make, Model:	
Microwave Make and Model:	
Television Make and Model:	
Stereo/Sound System Make Model:	
TV Roof Antennae Make and Model:	
WiFi Booster Make and Model:	
Additional Appliance:	

HVAC System Information

Furnace Make and Model:	
Air Conditioner Size, Make and Model:	
Ventilation Fans Make and Model:	
Air-Return Filters Size and Type:	
Thermostat Make and Model:	
NOTES:	

Safety Equipment

Smoke/CO Detector Make and Model:	
LP Alarm/Detector Make and Model:	
Fire Extinguisher Type, Make and Model:	
Additional safety equipment:	
Additional safety equipment:	

Coach Exterior Information

Awning Size, Make and Model:	
Door Lock Type, Make and Model:	
Electric Steps Make and Model:	
Tow Hitch Load Capacity, Make and Model:	
Other Exterior Equipment:	

Your RV Maintenance Record

This record is used in conjunction with the Small-RV Ninja book, which explains what should be noted in each category.

You can download a .pdf version of this document to print out or save on your computer at: www.beachnana.com/bonus-content-srvn .

Each time you perform service, repair, or replacement of an item on your RV, make a note of the date here.

Safety Equipment Maintenance

Fire Extinguisher	
Smoke/CO Detector	
LP Detector	
NOTES:	

RV Electrical System Maintenance

House Battery	
Inverter	
Solar Panels	
Generator	
NOTES:	

RV Plumbing System Maintenance

Water Heater	
Water Pump	
Black Holding Tank	
Gray Holding Tank	
Fresh Water Holding Tank	

Water Filter	
Sinks, Showers	
Toilet	
Macerator	
Dump Hose	
NOTES:	

RV HVAC System Maintenance

Furnace	
Furnace Filters	
Air Conditioner	
Air Conditioner Filters	
Return Filters	
Thermostat	

Ventilation Fans	
Fan Filters	
LP Tank and Regulator	
NOTES:	

Engine and Chassis Maintenance

Oil	
Oil Filter	
Coolant	
Air Filters	
DEF	
Battery	
Warranty Service	
Brakes	

Brake Fluid	
Transmission	
Transmission Fluid	
Windshield Wipers	
Windshield Wiper Fluid	
Automatic Levelers	
Tires	
Tire Pressure Monitoring System	
Automatic Steps	
Awning	
Back up Camera	
Tow Hitch and Connections	

RV Appliance Maintenance

Refrigerator/Freezer	
Microwave Oven	
Stove/Cook Top	
WiFi Extender	
Satellite Dish	
Television	
Stereo System	
NOTES:	

CPSIA information can be obtained
at www.ICGtesting.com
Printed in the USA
FSHW021252311220
77310FS

9 781791 780746